The Dictator

The Bloody History of Sudanese President Omar al-Bashir

William Webb

Minute Help Press

www.minutehelp.com

Table of Contents

Introduction

The African country of Sudan has had a
complicated and controversial history, filled with
endless civil wars and crimes against humanity.
Much of this controversy revolves around
Sudan's outspoken president, Omar Hassan
Ahmad al-Bashir, a Lieutenant General who has
been accused of genocide and war crimes by
the International Criminal Court. The controversy
over his tenure involves his efforts to improve
Sudan's economy, while having the country in a
dictatorial stranglehold that has made Sudan's
future questionable.

Chapter 1: Early Life and Education

Located in Northern Africa, Sudan is divided by
the Nile River. A mix of indigenous residents
from the Nile Valley and many who've migrated
from the Arabian Peninsula comprise the
majority of Sudan's population, with the country's
foremost religion being Islam.

Al-Bashir was born in the town of Hosh Bannaga, outside of the Sudanese capital, Khartoum on January 1, 1944. At the time he was born, Sudan was officially known as the Kingdom of Egypt and Sudan. His ancestry has been traced back to the Bedouin Al-Bedairyya Al Dahmashyya tribe, a Northern ethnic group, mainly consisting of Sudanese Arabs. At the time al-Bashir was born, Sudan was a political territory, or condominium, between the United Kingdom and Egypt.

There is very little information available regarding Al-Bashir's childhood, and not even the names of his parents have been made public, aside from reports that his father was a 'hallab', or one who milks cows. As for his education, al-Bashir received his primary education in the town of Shendi, which is situated on the eastern bank of the Nile River, and his secondary education in Khartoum, after his family relocated there. While in school he supported himself and paid for his own education by working in an automotive repair shop.

Military Career

Al-Bashir's military career started almost as soon as he graduated from school. In 1960, he entered the Sudanese Army, where he spent time at the Egyptian Military Academy in Cairo and did some training in Malaysia—he would eventually graduate as an officer from the Sudan Military Academy in 1966.

Al-Bashir then spent the next 26 years involved with the military. As a highly disciplined soldier, he ascended quickly to the esteemed position of officer in the paratrooper division. It is believed that he fought during the First Sudanese Civil War (1955-72), when the region of Sudan fought against the North for regional autonomy.

Both Northern and Southern Sudan had existed as separate territories, yet they had been merged together in the late 1940s as one country; Southern Sudan at the time had a primarily Christian population, whereas the North was primarily Muslim. When Egypt and the United Kingdom granted Sudan its independence, tensions escalated and war broke out between the two territories. The First Civil War lasted for almost 17 years, ending in 1972, with Southern Sudan becoming an autonomous region for the time being. Approximately half a million people died in the war.

Al-Bashir's military experience came in handy when he fought for Egypt during the Yom Kippur War against Israel in October 1973, a war that ended in two ceasefires. He then was selected to serve as the Sudanese military attaché in the United Arab Emirates in 1975, a position he held through 1979. During this period, al-Bashir was slowly becoming immersed in politics, involving himself in the National Islamic Front, which was founded by Hassan al-Turabi (al-Turabi would eventually become Sudan's Minister of Justice in 1979). With his extensive military background behind him, al-Bashir was selected as one of the leaders of the Islamist wing of the Sudanese Army.

After his time in Egypt, he served as a Garrison Commander in Khartoum in 1981, followed by six years as the commander of an armored parachute brigade. In the early 1980s, al-Bashir led several successful military assaults against the Sudan People's Liberation Army, eventually moving up through the ranks to serve as Commander of the 8th Brigade. It was in the late 1980s that he became a colonel.

The Rise of Islam and Political Issues in Sudan

A movement was underway in Sudan in the late 1960s and 1970s, a movement that eventually converted Sudan into an Islamist state. The Islamic Movement in Sudan originated in the late 1940s as a counterpart to Egypt's Islamic Brotherhood, a religious and social movement that had spread throughout the Arab world. Much of the organization's backbone was influenced by Sudanese students being introduced to the Brotherhood while studying in Egypt. With so many gradually being influenced by the Brotherhood's ideology, a conference took place in 1954 that officially established a Unified Muslim Brotherhood Organization in Sudan.

Splinter groups would be formed over time, the most notable being the Islamic Charter Front (ICM) in 1964. Led by scholar Hassan al-Turabi, he would become highly instrumental in transforming Northern Sudan towards the moral Islamic code of Sharia. The ICM eventually evolved into the National Islamic Front, the current leading political party in Sudan.

The NIF was unique in that it respected the rights of women and allowed them to run for political office, while at the same time it attempted to impose Islamic law nationwide. Under the leadership of al-Turabi, the Brotherhood gained enormous pull, especially amongst political groups and financial institutions, along with the Sudanese army.

The National Islamic Front has been a critical part of Sudan's history, dominating Sudan politics since 1989 by imposing a strict Islamic government that abides by Sharia law, which denies any form of secularism in Sudan's government. It was this installation of the National Islamic Front that helped spearhead a culture of violence in Sudan that continues through the present day.

The presidency of Ismail al-Azhari, who was the leader of the National Unionist Party, was overthrown in 1969 in a military coup led by Gaafar an-Nimeiry. Al-Azhari believed that having civilians in charge had corrupted the country, leaving Sudan to deal with numerous economical issues; he also felt that Sudan did not have a proper constitution, and had no sympathy for the Southern Sudanese, which his government frequently oppressed with military action. An-Nimeiry was a Sudanese Colonel who had led the Free Officers Movement and established the Sudanese Socialist Union, which existed as Sudan's only political party until 1985.

During his tenure as president, an-Nimeiry signed the Addis Ababa Agreement, which brought a ceasefire to the First Sudanese Civil War and self-governance to the Christian-based South. He proposed a new ideology, claiming Sudan to be a Socialist nation, which helped open the door to foreign investors, including oil companies.

An ally of the United States, an-Nimeiry eventually faced several abortive coup attempts by Sudanese Communists, yet with a single, one-party rule, he eventually capitulated to Northern demands and eventually transformed Sudan into an Islamist state under Sharia Law.

The South was infuriated by these developments, which inevitably led to a Second Sudanese Civil War. Many in retrospect see his time as leader prior to the start of the second war as relatively peaceful and economically prosperous.

During this time Al-Bashir was not only becoming politically motivated through his involvement with the National Islamic Front, but his extensive military background helped him become one of the leaders of the Islamist wing of the Sudanese Army, a position that attracted the attention of an-Nimeiry's State Security Organization.

An-Nimeiry himself would be removed from power by a coup in 1985, led by his own Defense Minister, Abdel Rahman Swar al-Dahab, who served as both Commander in Chief and Chairman of the Transitional Military Council. Al-Dahab's tenure would only last a year, as democratic elections were held in 1986 with Ahmed al-Mirghani becoming the next president. It would seem that al-Mirghani's government was more of a puppet leadership, as real power was apparently held by Sadiq al-Madhi, who was Sudan's prime minister.

Al-Madhi had spearheaded a coalition government comprised of the National Islamic Front, the Umma Party, the Democratic Unionists and minor parties based in the South. Al-Madhi was controversial for giving high-ranking political posts to members of his family and began a campaign to expel the entire Sudanese Communist party.

There was much speculation that al-Bashir was planning his own coup on behalf of the National Islamic Front. Al-Bashir was then transferred to the South Kordofan region of Northern Sudan, where it is believed that he, under the guidance of Sadiq al-Madhi, began to train ethnic militias so as to crush the Sudan People's Liberation Army (SPLA), a guerilla movement based in South Sudan. As mentioned before he was promoted to the rank of Brigadier in 1988, and continued to play an active role in the field.

1989 military coup

With the Second Sudanese Civil War in full swing, there was undeniable frustration within the country; close to 300,000 Sudanese had fallen victim to unspeakable famine throughout the country, and the country's economy was in dire straits. It is also believed that al-Madhi was planning to arrest several military officials, along with several civilians, who had been planning to restore deposed former president Gaafar an-Nimeiry back into power. With al-Bashir apparently at the helm, several military officers approached Prime Minister al-Madhi with a succinct choice: bring the Civil War to an end or al-Bashir and his team would step in and conclude the matter.

Needless to say there existed great instability during al-Mirgahni's tenure as president. The coalition government was constantly at odds with itself, which allowed al-Bashir to spearhead a coup on June 30, 1989, one that removed both al-Mirghani and al-Madhi from power. The coup was swift and effective.

Al-Turabi supported the coup, which ushered in a period of great violence. Many high-ranking members of the military were executed; opposing political parties were banned, as were independent newspapers. Many Sudanese politicians and journalists were also imprisoned for criticizing the government. Al-Bashir made a public announcement, boldly stating "I vow here to purge from our ranks the renegades, the hirelings, enemies of the people and enemies of the armed forces...Anyone who betrays the nation does not deserve the honor of living." After the alleged corruption of the previous administration, al-Bashir made a sweep of the sectarian population by purging the police and military, as well as the public sector, of any perceived opposition.

Once al-Bashir came to power, al-Turabi was placed under house arrest (he would be released shortly thereafter and continues to be involved in the National Islamic Front). Needless to say, amidst all the confusion, that with al-Bashir in power, an increasing rise in violence would plague Sudan for close to 25 years.

Chapter 2: Early Presidency

Al-Bashir would rule Sudan as leader of the Revolutionary Command Council for National Salvation (RCC), while also serving as Sudan's Minister of Defense. In the aftermath of the take over, al-Bashir appointed himself the civilian President of Sudan on October 16, 1993, and in the process dismantled the entire military organization that had helped him ascend to the presidency.

One of his first acts was to disband all political parties, especially the RCC, which enabled al-Bashir to enact the coup that brought him to power. He had originally served as the Council's Chairman in addition to serving as Prime Minister, Minister of Defense, and Commander of the Sudanese Armed Forces. Under the umbrella of the RCC al-Bashir was able to persecute any members of the opposition, as well as putting opposing newspapers out of business. Once al-Bashir claimed himself president, the executive and legislative powers of the RCC were given completely to al-Bashir, and from that point onward he would work to establish Sudan as an Islamic totalitarian single-party state.

It was also in 1993 that Sudan was added to the United States' list of nations that sponsor state terrorism. While it is believed that Sudan originally wanted to stop any form of terrorist activity, it became impossible with the escalation of the Second Sudanese Civil War. With the country's conversion to Conservative Islam, Sudan eventually became a breeding ground for terrorist organizations; for example, Osama Bin Laden came to Sudan in the early 1990s to build an al-Qaeda training camp and to seek funding for his organization.

Sudan has also had numerous links to other terrorist organizations, including Hezbollah, Hamas, the Palestinian Islamic Jihad and the Iranian Army of the Guardians of the Islamic Revolution, all of which have either used or established training camps in Sudan for the purpose of terrorist acts. Because of this, Sudan has been the recipient of numerous sanctions by the United Nations since 1996.

With one of the major reasons for the coup being Sudan's faltering economy, al-Bashir gave his administration the power to implement the Sudanese Dinar, replacing the existing currency, the Sudanese Pound, which had suffered greatly during the 1980s. While the Dinar is now obsolete at today's current exchange rate, 439.26 Dinar would be comparable to one US Dollar. (The Dinar was considered to be a highly volatile currency, meaning that its value was apt to change at a drastic rate; it would be replaced by the Sudanese Pound in 2007.)

Al-Bashir would eventually be re-elected to a five-year term in 1996. All of the major opposition parties in Sudan were boycotted, so al-Bashir was basically the only candidate to legally run for office. The once deposed al-Turabi was allowed to run for office, winning a seat in the Sudanese National Assembly where he would serve as its speaker.

Two years later, in 1998, al-Bashir worked with the Presidential Committee to draft a new Constitution. The end result greatly limited any form of political opposition to al-Bashir's now legally recognized political party, the National Congress Party (NCP), a nationalistic and conservative party that promotes Islam, very much in the manner of the National Islamic Front. The party also instituted Sharia Law throughout the country. The new Constitution would forbid the formation of any new political parties, therefore making any type of political opposition null and void. This would change once the Darfur Crisis came into question in the near future.

Despite the totalitarian and Islamist shift in Sudan's government, there clearly existed a power struggle between al-Bashir and al-Turabi. As a result, in December 1999 (right in the middle of the month-long Islamic religious observance of Ramadan), al-Bashir disbanded the parliament and did away with the constitution, while relieving al-Turabi of his position in the National Assembly. Al-Bashir then declared a state of emergency throughout Sudan and sent troops to control the parliament.

Al-Turabi criticized al-Bashir as being a tyrant and stated his actions were unconstitutional. It appeared as if al-Turabi was attempting to wield power from al-Bashir, especially when al-Turabi's party had a dominant control of parliament seats, yet both had apparently worked in conjunction together for many years, with al-Turabi providing political insight and al-Bashir offering military support.

What appeared to be even more damning for al-Bashir was the publication of the Black Book manuscript, a scathing indictment of injustice in Sudan that was published in two parts, in 2000 and 2002. The book elaborated on the gross imbalance of power in Sudan, especially in terms of the North's stranglehold over other regions of the country. The government was convinced that al-Turabi was behind the publication of the Black Book, though he denied any involvement. With Sudan having a firm grip on opposition publications, involving journalists and newspapers, the Black Book was published underground, mass-produced as photocopies and initially handed out publicly to individuals at mosques as they left after evening prayers.

In the aftermath of the Black Book scandal, and with the state of emergency still in place, the Sudanese parliament reconvened in early 2001 and al-Turabi was arrested for expressing sympathy with the Sudan People's Liberation Army, as well as threatening national security; he would spend the next four years incarcerated in a maximum security prison.

Chapter 3: Human Rights Abuses Under al-Bashir's Leadership

Women's Rights

Al-Bashir imposed tough restrictions on Northern Sudan's citizens. For example, music, dancing and wedding celebrations were all banned and the public flogging and beating of women became part of Sudan's laws in 1991.

Two instances of such beatings were made public, the first in 2009 involved Sudanese activist Lubna al-Hussein who was arrested for wearing trousers (which is considered indecent in Sudan), only to have her sentence commuted. Her case received worldwide attention, and she has since become an advocate for women's rights in Sudan.

Despite al-Hussein's notoriety and calling attention to her abuse, a horrific video appeared on the Internet in 2010 depicting a teenage girl being viciously beaten with a bullwhip for simply wearing a pair of pants. Another incident in 2012 involving a young woman being stoned for having a child out of wedlock and then imprisoned also caused an international uproar.

Similar to how Afghanistan was under the Taliban, women's rights under al-Bashir's rule have been incredibly strict. Women have no apparent legal right to ownership, including land. Women are expected to have their husbands handle their finances, since they are forbidden from any type of banking. Women also have very little freedom in terms of dress, as they are required to be completely covered in opaque ensembles, similar to a burqa. Women's rights are vastly different in Southern Sudan, where they are allowed to move freely and have some semblance of independence.

Slavery

Modern day slavery is epidemic in present day Sudan, which is seen as a form of oppression against the country's non-Muslim population. Numerous aid workers have claimed that up to 200,000 individuals have been sold into slavery, the majority of which are non-Muslim Africans (primarily women and children) who are sold to Muslim Arabs at rates of up to $50. Many former slaves have described unspeakable torture, excessive abuse and repeated rape at the hands of their masters.

Several international charity organizations have actually purchased individuals from modern day slave traders in an effort to free them from their captors. The Sudanese Embassy has repeatedly denied that slavery exists in Sudan, and that all accounts of slave trading are being made to portray Muslims in a negative light.

Freedom of the Press

Prior to al-Bashir's presidency, there were numerous publications available from Sudan's numerous political parties. Daily newspapers were abundant and available in both English and Arabic.

Once al-Bashir came to power, these publications were completely abolished and numerous journalists were arrested, most likely for criticism of al-Bashir. Since the 1989 coup, all newspapers and magazines, of which there are very few left, have been published and censored via government and military control, ensuring that all publications reflect a government perspective.

Several political papers, such as Al Hadaf (Sudanese Baath party), the Umma Party's Sawt Al Umma (Umma Party) and Al Midan (Communist based) have existed, but they are printed in underground circles and have limited distribution. Private run publications do exist in Sudan, but the government has great influence over what can be published or broadcast.

The government had initially been relentless in its persecution of journalists and has, over the years, made attempts to actually shut down several news-based websites (Sudanese Online and Hurriyat), whose focus often tends to be critical of al-Bashir and the government. Approximately 10% of the Sudanese population has access to the Internet.

Sudan also heavily controls its television industry. Since the coup of 1989, the Sudan National Broadcasting Corporation has operated through government control. Much of its broadcasting is Islamic based featuring government news that reflects national policy, as well as continuous recitations of the Koran.

Chapter 4: Civil War

The Second Sudanese Civil War has dominated the majority of al-Bashir's tenure as president. While the fighting broke out in 1983 prior to his takeover, many have seen both the First and Second Civil Wars as one long, drawn out war, with an 11-year cease-fire.

As mentioned before, the original cease fire that ended the First Civil War in 1972 allowed for the South to have a fair amount of religious and cultural autonomy. However, with the South having greater access to water, the North actively sought to control the whole country.

The causes of the war are many, with the primary one being a loss of autonomy in Southern Sudan, after president Gaafar An-Nimeiry's decision to turn Sudan into an Islamist state. Oil also came into play, as much of Sudan's oil production was based in the Southern part of the country (approximately 70% of Sudan's export profits), and the South also had greater access to water, whereas the North is largely composed of desert and borders the Sahara. Another issue was the government seizing private land and distributing it amongst Sudanese officials. Some critics believe that the war has its origins in centuries-long disputes over land and border disputes.

The South was represented by the Sudan People's Liberation Army (SPLA), a guerilla movement that had been formed by rebellious members of the Sudanese Army, led by John Garang de Mabior, who sought a more secular Sudan. Ethnic and religious issues have also been seen as a major cause of the ongoing war, with Muslim Arabs fighting against Christian Africans. These two Civil Wars have presented a great emotional and economic drain for Sudan.

In the aftermath of the first cease fire, which was signed in 1972 and implemented into the Sudanese Constitution, the agreement would eventually be violated, which would help spearhead the start of another Civil War. One of the first signs of trouble came when President Gaafar An-Nimeiry made an effort to seize all the oilfields along the North/South border, which meant that he would profit should he control them.

With Islamic Fundamentalism on the rise, it became apparent that there would be frustration with the South having its own autonomy as a Christian-based region. An-Nimeiry declared all of Sudan as Islamic in 1983, meaning that Southern Sudan no longer existed as its own region, yet An-Nimeiry assured that the rights of all non-Muslim citizens would be honored. Apparently this was not to be the case as rigid persecution of those in the South as well as those who were not Muslim continued, with these citizens being subjected to harsh treatment as imposed by the newly implemented Sharia Law.

Prime Minister Sadiq al-Mahdi attempted to negotiate peace with the SPLA in 1986, with the prime intention being to abolish Sharia Law. By 1988, a treaty was attempted between the SPLA and the Democratic Unionist Party (DUP), which would abolish Sharia Law and implement a cease-fire. This failed as al-Madhi refused to accept this peace plan and violence escalated as a result of the Sudanese economy raising prices on consumer goods. Sudanese citizens rioted in protest of these increases, which the government in response then cancelled.

Peace talks were in the works between the government and the SPLA, yet it was at this time that al-Bashir's coup took place, and he began implementing drastic measures to streamline the government of all opposition leaders and dissenters. Any peace agreement with the DUP was off the table, with al-Bashir's government stating that it would negotiate directly with the SPLA. Negotiations in late 1989 between the two sides broke no new ground, and the war continued.

The Criminal Act of 1991 was a penal code that inflicted incredibly strict penalties, including extreme cruelty, such as amputations. While the South was initially spared these penalties, it did not mean that the South would be exempt from such actions. The government first transferred non-Muslim judges from the South to the Northern part of Sudan and replaced them with Muslim judges, then created the Public Order Police force to ensure that Sharia Law was being practiced and followed in the North, leading to many penalties against non-practitioners.

Also, in 1991, Sudan had to contend with a drought that lasted for two years. To make matters worse, there was a food shortage. An international relief effort, Operation Lifeline Sudan (OLS), was launched in conjunction with the UN that would distribute close to 100,000 tons of food in an attempt to prevent starvation and help ease the suffering. Yet with the onset of the Gulf War in Iraq, and Sudan's support of Saddam Hussein's invasion of Kuwait, many nations withdrew their support. American investments in Sudan were prohibited; the Clinton administration, in response, funded African nations along Sudan's border to prevent possible invasions by Sudanese forces. It was at this time that Sudan was being referred to as a 'rogue state'.

It should be noted that Sudan relied on other nations for a majority of their weapons. The Soviet Union provided military training and weapons, such as tanks and aircraft during the First Civil War. China and Egypt both supplied a great number of weapons as well during the 1970s. In the late 1970s, the United States sold military equipment and weapons to Sudan in an effort to thwart incursions from Marxist African nations supported by the Soviet Union; military support from the US stopped around 1987. Iran supplied most of Sudan's weapons in the early 1990s, as well as providing close to 420 million in financial aid to Sudan.

One shocking aspect of the Civil War is that a large number of children, as young as 10 years old in some cases, were recruited to fight on both sides in numbers ranging up to 10,000. These children are, for the most part, abducted against their will and forced to clear mine fields, join suicide missions and fight on the front lines while heavily armed. Sudan has one of the worst records in regards to child soldiers, according to the Coalition to Stop the Use of Child Soldiers.

The Civil War not only became an endless struggle, but millions in the South would be displaced by the conflict, not to mention rampant starvation and a lack of health care. Many saw less compassion on behalf of al-Bashir's government in regards to the welfare of both Muslim and non-Muslims in Sudan, which in turn led to more sympathy towards the Southern rebels.

The SPLA had made gains in controlling several Sudanese provinces (there are 15 altogether in Sudan), including Bahr al Ghazal, parts of Darfur, Kurdufan, and Equatoria and sections of the Upper Nile and Blue Nile. However there was dissention among the rebels, and there were numerous splinter groups that appeared in an attempt to overthrow Colonel Garang. The breakaway groups joined forces and formed the SPLA United, which in turn led to tribal clashes between the different groups. The breakaway groups would eventually reconcile and rejoin forces with the SPLA.

The Northern Sudanese Armed Forces made headway and seized control of Southern Sudan in 1992 and captured the SPLA's headquarters. The unfortunate outcome of this offensive was the capturing of close to 200,000 citizens, including women and children from Southern Sudan, who were then sold into slavery.

A peace initiative known as the Intergovernmental Authority for Development (IGAD) was underway in 1993 with the intervention of Ethiopia, Eritrea, Kenya and Uganda. The IGAD helped spearhead the 1994 Declaration of Principles (DOP), an attempt at a peace settlement that would help improve the sharing of power and wealth between North and South and freedom of religion, while also giving the South the ability to create its own identity. The Sudanese government in Khartoum would eventually sign the agreement in 1997 after losing several battles to the SPLA.

Meanwhile, in 1995, opposition forces in the North sided with the rebels in the South to create a coalition of multiple parties, to be called the National Democratic Alliance, an organization that included representatives from the Umma Party, the Sudan People's Liberation Movement, the Communist Party of Sudan, and the Arab Baath Socialist Party, among several others. Troops from Eritrea, Ethiopia and Uganda arrived that same year to assist the SPLA in their fight against the North.

Despite the war going on, al-Bashir was re-elected as president in 1996, winning 75% of the vote.

The SPLA made headway by aligning themselves with several factions against the North. As mentioned before, The Khartoum Peace Agreement would be signed in 1997 between the National Islamic Front (NIF) in the North and militia organizations in the South, but was not seen as legally binding, since it was not signed by members of the SPLA. Yet even as the war continued and grew more violent, many saw this initial gesture as a fragile blueprint for the Peace Agreement that would eventually end the war.

In addition to the Khartoum agreements, the government and the rebels signed additional agreements that resembled the IGAD agreement, which would give the South the ability to be autonomous.

Other countries became involved in trying to broker a peace agreement. Egypt and Libya developed the Egypt-Libya Initiative (ELI) to bring all parties together; the initiative attempted to help establish an interim government in which dual power would be shared, as well as constitutional reform and free elections. The main problem was that it did not receive support from the SPLA as it did not address religious matters and there was no mention of self-autonomy. The National Democratic Alliance, which opposed al-Bashir, accepted the terms. Needless to say, the initiative failed.

In the 2000 presidential elections, al-Bashir was re-elected once again, receiving over 85% of the vote.

In 2001, John Danforth, a United States Senator, former US Ambassador to the United Nations, and an ordained Episcopal priest, entered talks with Sudan as a peace envoy. Danforth attempted to find ways that the US could help bring an end to the war, while at the same time helping improve humanitarian services to those who had suffered from the war's effects. Danforth was instrumental in helping to end violence between the Northern Muslims and the Southern Christian Rebels, yet in the end, his efforts would prove unsuccessful as fighting raged on for several more years.

On October 12, 2002, US President George W. Bush signed into law the Sudan Peace Act, which basically condemned Sudan for genocide. The act was also seen as a way to bring a close to the Civil War, while at the same time condemning all acts of violence on behalf of the government and the rebels. The act also condemned Sudan's record on human rights violations, their propensity to institute slavery and the murder of innocent civilians. The act authorized the use of $100 million to be used during a three-year time frame to help support the Sudanese people in areas outside of Sudan's control.

There was finally a breakthrough of sorts in 2002, as both sides came to the bargaining table in an agreement related to Southern Sudan's right to self-leadership. With intervention from Kenyan General Lazaro Sumbeiywo, representatives from the Sudanese government and the SPLA travelled to Machakos, Kenya for peace talks scheduled at different times over the course of a year. The Comprehensive Peace Agreement (CPA) was geared to end the war and implement nationwide democracy, while also sharing revenues from oil distribution. The agreement was signed on December 31, 2004.

The United Nations Security Council adopted this agreement, which emphasized an international effort to help both Sudan and Southern Sudan fulfill all articles of the CPA. The numerous agreements involved such subjects as the sharing of power, wealth, security issues and the implementation of an official ceasefire. In addition, it provided a schedule in which Southern Sudan was able to vote for its independence (this wouldn't occur until July 9, 2011, when Southern Sudan won its right to be its own nation, South Sudan).

After 22 years of fighting, which left approximately two million people dead, mainly due to drought and starvation, the Second Sudanese Civil War was officially over.

Chapter 5: Darfur conflict

As the Sudanese Civil War was nearing its end, another conflict began to dominate Sudan that would have a profoundly negative effect on al-Bashir's administration. The western province of Darfur has had a tumultuous history since 2003, when both the Sudan Liberation Army (SLA) and Justice and Equality Movement (JEM) attacked government targets and accused the government in Khartoum of oppressing black Africans over Arabs.

The actual cause of the war can be linked to land and grazing disputes between nomadic Arabs who sought access to land owned by farmers from numerous ethnic communities. The overall opinion is that the Arab population was persecuting Christians, in a move that has been compared to Apartheid in South Africa. An interesting aspect of this war is that a majority of Darfur's residents are actually Muslim.

The problem in Darfur began with small rebel attacks on local military outposts and police departments that were responded to with air and land attacks from the Khartoum government. The group, originally named the Darfur Liberation Front, eventually transformed into the Sudan Liberation Movement/Army (SLA), whose main function was to support and defend all of the oppressed people in Sudan.

As the rebels progressed with numerous raids, where they acquired vast quantities of weapons, President al-Bashir threatened to respond with military action, despite the fact that he was already fully engaged with the Sudanese Civil War. The rebels would prove difficult to confront, as the army was not properly trained to fight in the desert, yet the government responded with a vicious air assault.

One assault in particular that was led by both SLA and JEM forces drove into the town of al-Bashir and destroyed numerous airplanes and helicopters with close to 80 soldiers killed. Further victories by the rebels would prove to be embarrassing for al-Bashir's government. The SLA was quite relentless, leaving several hundred soldiers dead. To counteract the SLA the government enlisted members of the Janjaweed, a tribe of armed Arab cattle herders, to serve as a paramilitary force.

The strategy worked and the Janjaweed made military gains by killing several thousand non-Arab citizens of Darfur. As a result, a mass exodus of refugees numbering close to 100,000 fled Sudan for Chad, with which Sudan shares a border. The Janjaweed followed the refugees into Chad and engaged the Chadian army.

US Secretary of State Colin Powell met with al-Bashir in June 2004, where he demanded that al-Bashir allow humanitarian aid to come to Darfur. Al-Bashir apparently brushed Powell's recommendations aside; the US government was quick to claim that al-Bashir and the Janjaweed were responsible for what amounted to genocide and that there appeared to be no end in sight to the horrific crimes against civilians.

One month later Sudan was given an ultimatum by the United Nations to reign in the Janjaweed and disarm them. The issued Resolution 1556 threatened sanctions as well as an arms embargo against Sudan. Al-Bashir responded that Darfur was nothing more than a skirmish and that the United States and England should not meddle in Sudan's affairs.

There appeared a great disparity regarding villages and towns that were populated by Muslims and those by non-Muslims. The non-Muslim villages would often be raided and basically destroyed by the Janjaweed, while Muslim villages would be unscathed.

Aside from these battles, there were the first signs of peace negotiations when Chad became involved in a Humanitarian Ceasefire Agreement with the SLA, JEM and the Sudanese Government, which was not honored as attacks continued by the Janjaweed and the rebels. A ceasefire commission was established to monitor the situation with both Rwandan and Nigerian troops brought in to protect them.

Shortly thereafter, the United Nations issued a resolution claiming that Sudan was not fulfilling its part of the bargain by still implementing attacks against residents of Darfur. Members of the African Union were then brought in to monitor the situation.

Despite attempts to curb the violence, there were reports of inhumane crimes against the Darfuri that drew a close comparison to the ethnic cleansing in the Bosnian and Kosovo war and the genocide in Rwanda between the Hutus and Tutsis. Reports spread that the Darfuri were suffering such unspeakable treatment as the dismembering of limbs and the relentless murder of women and children. In regards to coverage of Darfur, al-Bashir's government has been extremely ruthless in preventing any news being made public. Reporters have been imprisoned and harassed and witnesses have been killed over the years, making it extremely difficult to get a full scope of the horrors of the genocide.

Al-Bashir issued a statement that the rebellion had been stopped in early 2004, yet that did nothing to stop raids and excessive violence in the area.

During a meeting in October 2004, the leaders of Chad, Egypt, Libya, Nigeria and Sudan discussed foreign intervention in the war. They agreed that the issue was solely an African issue and that the International community should provide assistance to Sudan in order to fulfill its part in the recent UN resolutions.

A January 2005 report by the International Commission of Inquiry on Darfur claimed that both the Sudanese government and the Janjaweed were responsible for perpetrating crimes such as murder, torture, wanton destruction of villages, forced displacement, rape and forced imprisonment (rape and sexual assault among women and girls by armed soldiers and militia members has almost become epidemic in Darfur). The report also added that all the violence had been committed against the African tribes in Darfur. The Commission had visited the region in late 2004 and held discussions with refugees and witnesses to the crimes. The Commission held back on referring to the excessive violence as genocide, yet it recommended that the International Criminal Court arrest those responsible and put them on trial.

In July of 2005, John Garang, the one time colonel of the SPLA became the vice-president of Sudan, yet his term was short lived as he died in a helicopter crash less than a month later. Many felt his role in the government would be instrumental in bringing an end to the situation in Darfur, and questions arose over whether his death was an accident or if he was in fact, murdered.

Things took a bizarre turn, also in 2005, when the government launched an attack on the country of Chad, in which close to 300 rebels were slaughtered in the city of Adré. The violence then led to the start of a war between Sudan and Chad.

In May of 2006, a peace agreement (known as the Abuja Agreement) was signed between Sudan and representatives of the SLA, which in turn was spearheaded by Deputy Secretary of State Robert Zoellick, who had spent three full days with the two sides to broker the deal. The main goal of the agreement was to break up the numerous militias, such as the Janjaweed, who were terrorizing the Darfuri and to bring the rebel factions into the Sudanese army, which would lead to the sharing of power. One of the signatories, Minni Minnawi, an SLA representative, met with President Bush after signing the agreement.

Yet this agreement did nothing to stop the flow of violence in Darfur. In the summer of 2006, fighting actually increased and horrific crimes against women, including beating and gang rapes were reported. Secretary-General of the United Nations Kofi Annan requested 18,000 international troops be sent to the region to help keep the peace. Sudan was against the implementation of the UN troops, to which the United States issued a stern warning, especially after al-Bashir claimed that Darfur would eventually be a 'graveyard' for the soldiers.

In response to Annan's remarks, al-Bashir issued a statement: "I swear that there will not be any international military intervention in Darfur as long as I am in power." He also claimed that Jewish organizations were responsible for all the negative, anti-Sudanese propaganda in the world.

The International Criminal Court in The Hague
was also taking notice of the atrocities in Darfur,
claiming that it had enough evidence available to
bring those responsible for these crimes to trial.
In the time between 2004 and 2006, the UN
Security Council had issued up to ten resolutions
regarding the situation in Darfur, all of which had
failed in terms of protecting civilians.

In August of 2006, a report was issued by the
International Rescue Committee that claimed
that the Janjaweed were largely responsible for
several hundred women that had been raped or
sexually assaulted in a Darfur refugee camp,
and that the Janjaweed were largely responsible
for humiliating women throughout the region.

In late August a new resolution was passed by the UN, which would send 17,300 international troops to Darfur. Sudan was against this, and began a military offensive, followed by a warning that the African Union forces, who were reported to be ill-equipped in terms of both funding and equipment, were to leave Darfur by the end of September and that the United Nations had no right to interfere. The president of neighboring Chad, Idriss Deby, expressed support for the UN forces, while al-Bashir was strongly opposed to the plan, comparing it to the US invasion of Iraq. Al-Bashir initiated a major offensive in Darfur the day after the resolution was approved.

In September of 2006, then British Prime Minister Tony Blair composed an open letter to the members of the European Union, calling for them to side with the African Union and the United States in an attempt to solve the crisis. Blair added that the Darfur crisis was unacceptable, and that it was important for the European Union to play a role in changing the world's perspective on the situation.

While awaiting the arrival of UN forces, the situation in Darfur was becoming dire. As Sudan was continuously bombing and killing civilians, a humanitarian crisis was rapidly developing. Food relief organizations claimed that supplies were not reaching those in need, making the situation even more critical; the Food and Agriculture Organization ranked Darfur as the most crucial emergency in its annual report.

With international pressure coming from other countries, specifically Nigeria, to allow UN intervention, al-Bashir flatly refused. More sanctions against Sudan were imposed with the Darfur Peace and Accountability act, signed by President Bush in 2006. The act not only reinforced the US declaration of Sudan's actions as genocide and offered support for the International Criminal Court to file criminal charges against those involved, it also forbid American citizens from being involved in any transactions involving Sudan's oil reserves. The United States further added that it would have an international plan to solve the crisis, which the Sudanese Government would likely accept.

An announcement was made in November 2006 that the Sudanese government was willing to negotiate with the National Redemption Front (NRF), a conglomeration of the JEM, SLM and the Sudan Federal Democratic Alliance (SFDA), despite the belief that a new agreement was not necessary. Around the same time the Popular Forces Troops (PFT), a militia of Darfuri Arabs, was formed and announced that they had successfully thwarted an attack by Sudanese troops. They claimed that the Janjaweed did not represent the Arab population and that they were nothing more than violent thugs. The PFT were opposed to the war and aligned themselves with the rebel factions.

The UN Commissioner for Human Rights further accused the Sudanese government of an attack in Serbia in November 2006, in which 30 civilians were believed to have died.

In light of the severe brutality of the Sudanese army and the apparent failure of the United Nations to have any effect in stopping the genocide in Darfur, the Save Darfur Coalition was formed in 2004 during an emergency summit in New York City to call attention to the situation. Comprised of numerous international humanitarian, religious and political organizations, the organization helped to expose the world to what was really transpiring between the Sudanese government and Darfur. Many well-known figures attached themselves to the cause, including Holocaust survivor and Nobel Peace Prize-winner Elie Wiesel and actors Mia Farrow, Angelina Joie, Jonah Hill, Salma Hayek, Don Cheadle and George Clooney. It should be noted that Clooney has been one of the most outspoken advocates for ending the war in Darfur, even travelling to Sudan and Chad to expose the horrors experienced by Durfari refugees. He has used his personality to meet with numerous world leaders, including German

Chancellor Angela Merkel and US President Barack Obama. As recently as 2012, he was arrested outside the Sudanese Embassy during a protest against the war.

In early 2007, it was announced that a tentative, sixty-day cease-fire was in the works between the government and the rebels, after talks between al-Bashir and former US Ambassador to the United Nations and (at the time) New Mexico Governor Bill Richardson. It was stressed that great attention would be paid during the cease-fire to address the humanitarian situation. Yet the cease-fire never fully took hold, as African Union peacekeepers were reported to have been killed by government forces. The United Nations would eventually accuse Sudan of perpetrating crimes against humanity in Darfur and requested immediate action to stop the violence. Kofi Anan held a meeting with al-Bashir and insisted that the Janjaweed be reigned in to stop any further violence.

In addition to Darfur, the war between Sudan and Chad was becoming more problematic as members of the Janjaweed launched an attack in which they circled the villages of Marena and Tiero and massacred roughly 400 people. According to reports, the majority of the victims were men, while the women in the villages were assaulted and robbed; other victims succumbed to dehydration while escaping.

President Bush threatened trade sanctions against al-Bashir's government if the attacks did not stop. As a result of the violence in both Chad and Darfur, The International Criminal Court, at the urging of ICC Chief Prosecutor Luis Moreno-Ocampo, filed charges against Ahmed Haroun (Sudan's human affairs minister) and a Janjaweed militia leader named Ali Kushyab with 51 counts of crimes against humanity. Haroun responded to the charges, claiming that was not guilty; he later led an investigation into human rights abuses in Darfur, where he appeared to prevent all relief efforts. He has never been arrested.

In the spring of 2007, al-Bashir and the President of Chad, Idriss Deby both signed an agreement (with the intervention of Saudi Arabia) in an effort to bring peace to the region. Many experts doubted that this new agreement would make any headway, especially since Chad itself had been engaged in its own war against rebel factions since 2006.

As the humanitarian crisis worsened, many organizations removed themselves from Darfur, claiming excessive violence against aid workers. Violence against these individuals had increased at an alarming rate, including the murder of a volunteer from a religious organization.

The African Union and United Nations joined forces to create the Hybrid Operation in Darfur (UNAMID) in July 2007, a joint peacekeeping initiative that was intended to help stabilize Darfur, while at the time planning out a peace agreement. Approximately 26,000 soldiers and military were sent to the area starting in October 2007, which incorporated the 9,000 forces of the African Union Mission in Sudan (AMIS). The soldiers coming from countries around the world, including Australia, Bolivia, Canada, China, France, Germany, Ireland, Italy, Nepal, Norway, Sweden, the United Kingdom and the United States, were given the green light to use force to help protect humanitarian aid workers as well as Darfuri civilians. The original goal of the initiative was to last for a twelve-month period, yet the resolution has been amended several times since it was officially passed. One hundred forty nine UNAMID peacekeepers have been killed in Darfur, as of April 2013.

While waiting for the deployment of the UNAMID Forces, several of the Sudanese rebel groups gathered for a conference in Tanzania. The main goal was how to approach peace negotiations with al-Bashir's government. While not all rebel leaders attended, they did draw a consensus that would allow for the sharing of power and wealth, that Darfur should be an autonomous region and that the victims of the war should be compensated for their suffering.

Several Arab tribes aligned with the Janjaweed, such as the Terjem and the Mahria, eventually broke off and formed their own splinter groups. These small groups were involved in additional skirmishes in late August 2007, but were not reported to be creating as much havoc.

Further peace talks were scheduled for late October 2007 in Libya. Representatives from the JEM splinter groups, the Revolutionary Democratic Forces Front, United Revolutionary Force Front, the Sudan Liberation Movement–G19, and the Sudan Federal Democratic Alliance attended, while the Justice and Equality Movement (who objected to the many rebel groups' presence at the conference) splinter groups from the Sudan Liberation Movement and a representative from the Darfuri Fur tribe refused to participate. With not all rebel factions willing to attend, the conference was seen as more of a preliminary phase of talks, with the hope of additional meetings to come.

An interesting turn of events transpired in November 2007 when nine of the rebel organizations, the Democratic Popular Front, the six branches of the SLM, the Sudanese Revolutionary Front and the Field Revolutionary Command branch of the JEM, signed a Charter of Unification, which would combine all the groups under the umbrella of the SLM. A further development followed later that month when Darfuri rebels formed two large groups in an effort to negotiate with al-Bashir.

Further fighting was reported in early 2008 as Sudan, joined by Arab militias, launched an offensive against rebels in Darfur near the border with Chad. Fighting wasn't only restricted to Darfur, as a major battle between the JEM and al-Bashir's forces took place in Omdurman, which is Sudan's largest city and located close to the capital, Khartoum. The rebels had travelled close to 1,000 miles from Darfur to launch the attack, which Al-Bashir quickly repelled. The end result left close to 100 soldiers and roughly 30 civilians dead; the rebels apparently suffered major losses and a curfew was established in Khartoum as a result.

In June 2008, al-Bashir gave an interview with British Journalist David Frost, where he boldly stated that no more than 10,000 people had died during the War in Darfur. Al-Bashir also stated during the discussion, that he refused to negotiate with JEM, claiming that peace was not their main goal.

In August of 2009, General Martin Agwai who was the top ranking official of UNAMID, claimed that the war in Darfur was officially over and that the main issue at the moment was security problems involving problems with bandits and disputes over land and water. It appeared as if fighting was on the wane, yet there were reports from aid workers that the violence was fairly consistent. Agwai added that the major problem in Darfur was political, yet no real peace agreement had been reached and rebel unification was still problematic.

By the end of 2010 talks were underway once again to try to bring an end to the war. Members of the Liberation and Justice Movement (the LJM, a coalition for several Darfuri rebel groups) met with representatives of al-Bashir's government in Doha, Qatar. Other groups, such as the Sudanese Alliance Resistance Forces in Darfur as well as the JEM were also involved in negotiations. While Darfuri autonomy and the creation of a Vice-Presidential office for the region were some of the issues discussed, neither side made any headway with a peace agreement. It should also be noted that in 2010 the war between Sudan and Chad finally came to an end; both sides signed an agreement that called for peace between both countries.

Yet there were promising signs in early 2011 as Tijani Sese, leader of the LJM, claimed that his group had agreed to the main proposals of the Doha conference. The conditions included up to three hundred million dollars as compensation for the victims and tribunals to prosecute those accused of atrocities. Plans were also drafted for a Darfuri Regional Authority that would have its own government for a period of five years, not affecting Darfur's existing states or provinces (North Darfur, South Darfur, and West Darfur).

An additional meeting on the Doha conference was planned for February 5, 2011. The LJM and the JEM both announced that they were still planning to participate in the negotiations, yet al-Bashir's government claimed that a peace plan could be enacted internally, without any involvement from the rebels. Sudan was equally committed to participate in negotiations, yet problems arose when the LJM and JEM eventually rejected the Doha peace agreement, with compensation and the Vice-Presidential option being the main issues.

In March, al-Bashir planned to create two additional states in Darfur (Central and Eastern Darfur), which, the rebels feared, would undermine their influence and allow more direct control from the government. A spokesman from the SLA, Ibrahim al-Helwu said this was nothing new in regards to al-Bashir's attempt to divide Darfur even further along tribal lines in an effort to make the region weak.

Another attempt to broker peace between al-Bashir's government and the rebels took place again in Doha, Qatar, which led to the signing of the 2011 Darfur Peace Agreement. Both the LJM and al-Bashir's government signed the agreement on July 11. The stipulations involved the creation of a fund to help Darfur's victims, gave al-Bashir the ability to designate a Darfuri Vice President and allowed for the creation of a Darfur Regional Authority, which would monitor Darfur until elections would be held to decide Darfur's permanent status. National power sharing was also part of the plan, allowing for each state in Darfur to nominate federal ministers as well as members to the Sudanese legislature. A problem arose as the referendum was postponed several days prior to it taking place and for at least another year.

The peace agreement did nothing to stop the swell of violence in Darfur, which has increased greatly since the Doha agreement was signed. As of April 2013 members of the SLA and the JEM were reported to be planning a full-scale assault on Khartoum in an attempt to take over the country.

While al-Bashir claimed that no more than 10,000 people have died in Darfur, the figures from International groups claim the numbers to be much higher. The United Nations believed that up to 300,000 people had died in the war and that the fighting had displaced over two million people. The World Health Organization reported that up to 70,000 people had died from starvation in the time frame from March to October 2004. Since the war began some observers claim that 10,000 people have died each month from starvation and lack of proper necessities. The refugee situation, mainly Darfuri escaping into Chad, had reached a number of close to three million people. However, there has been controversy over the actual statistics as the majority of the victims have died from malnutrition and lack of proper facilities as opposed to actual violence. As of June 2013, the war in Darfur still continues.

The majority of the International community has overwhelmingly condemned al-Bashir and the situation in Darfur. What has been controversial is the labeling of the war in Darfur as an actual act of genocide, as many groups and individuals have differing opinions. Organizations such as the US Holocaust Memorial Museum, the Anti-Defamation League, the Genocide Intervention Network, Physicians for Human Rights, the Armenian Assembly of America, the American Jewish Committee and the Jacob Blaustein Institute for the Advancement of Human Rights, as well as notable politicians as George W, Bush, Colin Powell, John Kerry, Joseph Lieberman, Russell Feingold, Hillary Clinton and Barack Obama, as well as the aforementioned actors, have considered the situation as genocide.

The United Nations did not consider the situation in Darfur to be genocide, despite extensive violence perpetrated by the Janjaweed. The African Union admitted that there were human rights abuses, but it was not tantamount to genocide. The medical organization Médecins Sans Frontières (Doctors Without Borders) felt that while there was a crucial humanitarian crisis in Darfur, it didn't account as genocide.

While there is some confusion on how to categorize the Darfur situation, it has become, according to some, as so dire that there appears to be no end in sight.

Chapter 6: Arrest Warrant

Despite the ongoing debate on whether to classify Darfur as genocide, the International Criminal Court (ICC), based in The Hague in the Netherlands, filed an arrest warrant against al-Bashir for war crimes, crimes against humanity and individual criminal responsibility for genocide on July 14, 2008.

Established in 1998, the ICC's origins date back to the Paris Peace conference of 1919 and the League of Nations (a precursor to the United Nations), when there was a call for a tribunal to prosecute individuals accused of committing atrocities. The idea was brought up again in the aftermath of the Holocaust in World War Two and lingered for decades, until an International Tribunal was established to prosecute those responsible for ethnic cleansing during the wars in Kosovo and Bosnia (both once part of Yugoslavia). Many cases have been brought before the ICC involving situations in the Democratic Republic of the Congo, the Central African Republic, Afghanistan, Honduras, Palestine, North Korea, Kenya, Libya, Côte d'Ivoire, Iraq, Venezuela and Mali.

What has made the ICC's arrest warrant of al-Bashir so unprecedented was that the court had never before brought charges against a sitting head of state. The main argument against al-Bashir was his complicity in planning the elimination of Darfur's three main ethnic groups: the Fur, the Masalit and the Zaghawa, by using rape, murder and forced deportation.

The official arrest warrant was issued on March 4, 2009, in which al-Bashir was indicted on five counts of crimes against of humanity, as well as two counts of war crimes, which involved the raids against Darfuri civilians. There was a conflict within the court, as it had officially ruled that the evidence in which to prosecute al-Bashir for genocide was insufficient; three judges on the court issued a dissent stating that there were enough grounds to prosecute him for genocide.

Another issue before the court was that since Sudan was not a party of the ICC, it therefore did not have to comply with issuing the warrant, yet the UN had passed a resolution in 2005 that required Sudan to comply with International Law. Other groups, such as Amnesty International insisted that Sudan comply with the ICC and that al-Bashir either voluntarily turn himself in or that the Sudanese government present him to ICC officials.

The enacting of the arrest warrant was problematic as the Sudanese Constitution allows the president immunity for any kind of prosecution during his or her term in office. The African Union and Arab League condemned the ICC warrant. Then President of Libya Muammar Gaddafi saw the arrest warrant as an act of terrorism and that the West was attempting to recolonize all of Africa; the Organization of the Islamic Conference and the Arab League also criticized the warrant as unacceptable.

The warrant did nothing to stop al-Bashir from visiting countries such as Chad, Egypt and Qatar, all of which refused to arrest him, especially despite al-Bashir's forces attacking soldiers in Chad. The Sudanese air force even went so far as to claim that they would protect al-Bashir from arrest, even while flying in International Airspace.

Al-Bashir denied the charges against him, claiming that all the accusations were nothing more than lies. In response to the warrant, al-Bashir ordered several aid organizations, such as Solidarities, Mercy Corps and Oxfam, expelled from Sudan, claiming that they were working as spies for foreign countries. UN Secretary General Ban Ki-moon heavily criticized Sudan's actions, and representatives from Oxfam denied any involvement in spying, further adding that their stand in International matters has always been impartial, and that their expulsion would harm up to 600,000 Sudanese in need of assistance.

Al-Bashir ran for president again in 2010, the first time that opposition parties (69 altogether) were allowed to run since al-Bashir took power in 1989. Winning with 68% of the vote, many of his opponents cried foul, claiming the election was rigged, especially after a video surfaced showing election officials illegally stuffing ballot boxes, which al-Bashir's government stated was fake.

There were reports of scattered violence throughout the election; several members of Sudan's ruling party were killed in a shootout and there were numerous reports that several districts suffered from manipulation and intimidation, even though the actual voting was supervised in part by former US President Jimmy Carter and members of the European Union.

Conclusion

In July of 2010, the ICC issued a second arrest warrant against al-Bashir, which added three counts of genocide to the pre-existing warrant issued in 2008. The ICC had spent the greater part of a year attempting to add the genocide charges to the warrant against him. The second warrant accused al-Bashir of involvement in the ethnic cleansing of the Fur, Masalit and Zaghawa tribes, and that according to the ICC, al-Bashir intentionally sought to destroy these tribes by using torture, rape and murder. In response, al-Bashir denied the charges against him. Over one hundred countries have avoided any interactions with al-Bashir, yet there still remains the issue of certain countries that are part of the ICC which have refused to arrest him.

The arrest warrants have clearly hampered al-Bashir's reputation throughout the world and with his lack of movement to other countries greatly impaired, only time will tell if he will ever have to answer for the crimes that he has been accused of.

Bibliography

Abdelaziz, Khalid, Laessing, Ulf and Lyon, Alistair. Sudan Security Bans Communist Newspaper. The Huffington Post. 2 June 2013. <http://www.huffingtonpost.com/2013/06/02/suda n-security-communist-newspaper_n_3374249.html?utm_hp_ref=media >

Al-Bashir, Omar. Frost, David. *Frost Over the World.* Al Jazeera. 20 June 2008.

"Alliance of rebel factions agrees to Darfur peace deal." Monsters and Critics. 3 January 2011. <http://news.monstersandcritics.com/africa/news /article_1609145.php/Alliance-of-rebel-factions-agrees-to-Darfur-peace-deal>

"Arab leaders snub al-Bashir warrant." Al
Jazeera. 31 March 2009
<http://www.aljazeera.com/news/middleeast/200
9/03/2009330175846714662.html>

"Blair's Darfur letter in full." BBC News. 17
September 2006.
<http://news.bbc.co.uk/2/hi/uk_news/politics/535
3348.stm>

"Chad fight back 'kills 300 rebels'." BBC News.
20 December 2005.
<http://news.bbc.co.uk/2/hi/africa/4544352.stm>

"Child soldiers in the firing line." BBC News. 8
April 2001.
<http://news.bbc.co.uk/2/hi/1266534.stm>

Cowell, Alan. "Military Coup In Sudan Ousts Civilian Regime." The New York Times. 1 July 1989. <http://www.nytimes.com/1989/07/01/world/military-coup-in-sudan-ousts-civilian-regime.html>

"Curfew in capital as Sudanese army clash near Khartoum with Darfur rebels." Sudan Tribune. 10 May 2008. <http://www.sudantribune.com/spip.php?article27076>

"Darfur war crimes suspect defiant." BBC News. 28 February 2007. <http://news.bbc.co.uk/2/hi/africa/6404467.stm>

"EXCLUSIVE: Darfur new rebel group announces formation of its structure." Sudan Tribune. 3 March 2010. <http://www.sudantribune.com/EXCLUSIVE-Darfur-new-rebel-group,34301>

"FACTBOX-Who is attending Darfur talks, who is not." Sudan Tribune. 27 October 2007. <http://www.sudantribune.com/spip.php?article2 4453>

Fiedler, Anke, Wollenberg, El Gizouli, Magdi and Deckert, Roman. The Sudanese press after separation – Contested identities of journalism. Berlin: Media in Cooperation and Transition, 2012

"Forty countries face food shortages, with Darfur the most pressing crisis: UN agency." UN News Centre. 9 October 2006. <http://www.un.org/apps/news/story.asp?NewsI D=20176&Cr=&Cr1=Food#.Ubnty0JgPHg>

Heavens, Andrew. "Darfur to be cut into smaller states; rebel protest." Reuters. 8 March 2011. <http://www.reuters.com/article/2011/03/08/ozat p-sudan-darfur- idAFJOE7270CL20110308?sp=true>

Hoge, Warren. "Sudan Flying Arms to Darfur, Panel Reports." The New York Times. 18 April 2007. <http://www.nytimes.com/2007/04/18/world/afric a/18sudan.html?n=Top%2fNews%2fWorld%2fC ountries%20and%20Territories%2fSudan&_r=0>

"ICC issues arrest warrant for Sudanese President al Bashir." Amnesty International. 4 March 2009. <http://www.amnesty.org/en/news-and-updates/news/icc-issues-arrest-warrant-sudanese-president-al-bashir-20090304>

International Criminal Court (ICC). *Report to the International Commission of Inquiry on Darfur to the United Nations Secretary-General*. 25 January 2005. <http://www.un.org/News/dh/sudan/com_inq_dar fur.pdf>

Kessler, Glenn. "Sudanese, Rebels Sign Peace Plan For Darfur." The Washington Post. 6 May 2006. <http://www.washingtonpost.com/wp-dyn/content/article/2006/05/05/AR2006050500305.html>

Lewis, Paul. "U.N. Criticism Angers Charities Buying Sudan Slaves' Release." The New York Times. 12 March 1999. <http://www.nytimes.com/1999/03/12/world/un-criticism-angers-charities-buying-sudan-slaves-release.html>

Malik, Nesrine. "Sudan's public order laws are about control, not morality." The Guardian. 11 December 2010. <http://www.guardian.co.uk/commentisfree/2010/dec/11/sudan-laws-control-not-morality>

"Nigerian FM arrives in Khartoum for talks on Darfur." People's Daily Online. 12 October 2006. <http://english.people.com.cn/200610/12/eng200 61012_311117.html>

"Nine Darfur rebel factions reunite under one structure." Sudan Tribune. 15 November 2007. <http://www.sudantribune.com/spip.php?article2 4751>

"No Western troops in Darfur – president." Iol News. 21 June 2006. <http://www.iol.co.za/news/africa/no-western-troops-in-darfur-president-1.282451#.UcEmGEJgPHg>

"Omar al-Bashir - Fast Facts." CNN. 10 December 2012. <http://www.cnn.com/2012/12/10/world/africa/om ar-al-bashir---fast-facts>

"Omar Hassan Ahmad al-Bashir." <u>Sudan</u>
<u>Tribune</u>. No Date Given.
<http://www.sudantribune.com/spip.php?mot126
>

Osman El-Tom, Abdullah. "Black Book of Sudan:
Imbalance of power and wealth in Sudan."
<u>Internet Archive</u>. No Date Given.
<http://web.archive.org/web/20080516091953/htt
p://www.ossrea.net/publications/newsletter/oct02
/article9.htm>

Parameswaran, P. "US threatens Sudan after
UN resistance." <u>Iol News.</u> 19 August 2006.
<http://www.iol.co.za/news/africa/us-threatens-
sudan-after-un-resistance-
1.290112#.Ubkv6EJgPHg>

"President Bashir, you are hereby charged…"
<u>The Scotsman.</u> 14 July 2008.
<http://www.scotsman.com/news/president-
bashir-you-are-hereby-charged-1-1080406>

"Profile: Omar al Bashir." The Telegraph. 5
March 2009.
<http://www.telegraph.co.uk/news/newstopics/pr
ofiles/4944799/Profile-Omar-al-Bashir.html>

"Profile: Sudan's President Bashir." BBC News.
25 November 2003.
<http://news.bbc.co.uk/2/hi/africa/3273569.stm>

"Q&A: Sudan's Darfur conflict." BBC News. 23
February 2010.
<http://news.bbc.co.uk/2/hi/africa/3496731.stm>

"Sadig Al-Madhi." Club Madrid. No Date Given.
<http://web.archive.org/web/20071008113131/htt
p://www.clubmadrid.org/cmadrid/index.php?id=3
97>

"Sharia Law and Women." Muslim Women's
Coalition. No Date Given.
<http://www.mwcoalition.org/quotas/id10.html>

"Signing of Doha Agreement prompts mixed reactions." <u>Radio Dabanga.</u> 15 July 2011. <http://www.radiodabanga.org/node/16328>

Simon, Marlise. "International Court Adds Genocide to Charges Against Sudan Leader." <u>The New York Times.</u> 12 July 2010. <http://www.nytimes.com/2010/07/13/world/afric a/13hague.html?_r=0>

"Situations and cases." <u>International Criminal Court.</u> No Date Given. http://www.icc-cpi.int/en_menus/icc/situations%20and%20case s/Pages/situations%20and%20cases.aspx

"Struggle to salvage Darfur talks." <u>BBC News.</u> 29 October 2007. <http://news.bbc.co.uk/2/hi/africa/7066792.stm>

"Sudan ex-rebel joins government." <u>BBC News.</u> 10 July 2005.

<http://news.bbc.co.uk/2/hi/africa/4666701.stm>

"Sudan opposition claims video shows election fraud." BBC News. 20 April 2010.
<http://news.bbc.co.uk/2/hi/africa/8633162.stm>

"Sudan orders aid agency expulsions." CNN. 4 March 2009.
<http://www.cnn.com/2009/WORLD/africa/03/04/sudan.expel/>

"Sudan: Palace Coup." The Economist. 16 December 1999.
<http://www.economist.com/node/327475>

"Sudan Peace Watch--December 21, 2010." Enough Project. 21 December 2010.
http://www.enoughproject.org/publications/sudan-peace-watch-december-21-2010>

"Sudan 'poll shooting' kills nine." Al Jazeera. 15 April 2010.

<http://www.aljazeera.com/news/africa/2010/04/
2010415883436865.html>

"Sudan Profile." <u>BBC News.</u> 7 November 2012.
<http://www.bbc.co.uk/news/world-africa-
14095119>

"Sudan Second Civil War 1983-2004." <u>Global
Security.org</u>. No Date Given.
<http://www.globalsecurity.org/military/world/war/
sudan-civil-war2.htm>

SUDAN: The case against Bashir. <u>Irin</u>. 4 March
2009.
<http://www.irinnews.org/report/83299/sudan-
the-case-against-bashir>

Thurston, Alex. "Sudan's Islamic Movement Heads to Its General Conference." Sahel Blog. 14 November 2012. <http://sahelblog.wordpress.com/2012/11/14/sudans-islamic-movement-heads-to-its-general-conference/>

U.S. Congress. 107th Congress Public Law 245. *Sudan Peace Act.* Washington, D.C. Government Printing Office, 2002 (f:publ245.107)

"UNAMID Facts and Figures." United Nations Peacekeeping. No Date Given. <http://www.un.org/en/peacekeeping/missions/unamid/facts.shtml>

"UNICEF adviser says rape in Darfur, Sudan continues with impunity". UN News Centre. 19 October 2004. <http://www.un.org/apps/news/story.asp?NewsID=12280&Cr=darfur&Cr1=>

"UN resolution on Darfur: Full text." <u>BBC News.</u>
30 July 2004.
<http://news.bbc.co.uk/2/hi/africa/3940527.stm>

"War in Sudan's Darfur 'is over'." <u>BBC News.</u> 27
August 2009.
<http://news.bbc.co.uk/2/hi/africa/8224424.stm>

"World Report 2011: Chad." <u>Human Rights
Watch</u>. No Date Given.
<http://www.hrw.org/en/world-report-2011/chad>

Printed in Poland
by Amazon Fulfillment
Poland Sp. z o.o., Wrocław